The Passion Principles

101 Ways to Express Your Creativity and Share It With the World

Bob Baker

Spotlight Publications
St. Louis, MO

www.PromoteYourCreativity.com

The Passion Principles

Published by Spotlight Publications and www.PromoteYourCreativity.com
PO Box 28441, St. Louis, MO 63146 USA
(314) 329-1395 • bob@bob-baker.com

Cover design: Tamara Dever, TLC Graphics, www.tlcgraphics.com

ISBN: 978-1548530846

Disclaimer

This book is designed to provide information and inspiration for musicians, writers, artists, and other creative people. It is sold with the understanding that the publisher and author are not engaged in rendering legal, accounting, or other professional services. If legal or other expert assistance is required, the services of a competent professional should be sought.

It is not the purpose of this book to cover the full range of information that is otherwise available on this topic, but instead to complement, amplify, and supplement other texts. You are urged to read all available material and tailor the information to your individual needs.

Every effort has been made to make this book as accurate as possible. However, there may be mistakes, and some details may be inaccurate by the time you read this. Therefore, this text should be used only as a general guide and not as the ultimate source of information on the topic.

The author and publisher shall have neither liability nor responsibility to any person or entity with respect to any loss or damage caused, or alleged to have been caused, directly or indirectly, by the information contained in this book.

Free Gifts for You!

As a special thank you for purchasing this book, I want to give you free access to my course, "30 Ways to Become an Empowered Artist."

You'll get more than three hours of online video training that will help you become a more confident and prosperous artist.

I'll also send you a free sample of my book, *The DIY Career Manifesto: The Unconventional Guide to Turning Your Talents and Know-How Into a Profitable Business*.

Just head to this website to claim these free gifts now:

www.PromoteYourCreativity.com

About the Author

Bob Baker is on a mission to help musicians, authors, and creative entrepreneurs of all kinds use their talents and know-how to make a living and make a difference in the world.

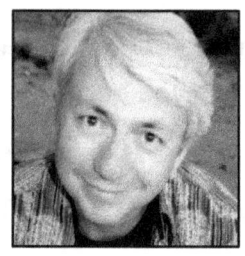

He is the author of the highly acclaimed *Guerrilla Music Marketing Handbook* and many other books, including *The Empowered Artist*, *The DIY Career Manifesto*, *Unleash the Artist Within*, and *Branding Yourself Online*.

He developed the "Music Marketing 101" course at Berkleemusic, the online education division of Berklee College of Music.

Bob is an active musician, workshop leader, visual artist, actor, and former music magazine editor who educates creative people how to get exposure, connect with fans, and increase their incomes through their artistic passions.

He also teaches and performs improv comedy and co-wrote *The Improv Comedy Musician* with Laura Hall, the longtime pianist and musical director of *Whose Line Is It Anyway?*

Since 1995 Bob has published "The Buzz Factor" ezine, one of the first music tips email newsletters in existence. He was one of the early proponents of musicians, writers, and other creative people taking their careers into their own hands and not relying on industry gatekeepers to save them.

Visit **www.Bob-Baker.com** for more info.

Contents

Introduction

Welcome to a little book filled with a multitude of powerful ideas.

If you're a musician, writer, visual artist, actor, designer, chef, performer, or any other type of creative entrepreneur, you'll find a feast of bite-sized principles throughout these pages.

By design, this book does not go in depth with career strategies or business tactics. Its purpose is to provide you with a comprehensive collection of the best nuggets of wisdom for artists of all kinds.

These are the philosophies and activities that the most successful creative people embrace. You'd do well to consider them and incorporate them into your own life.

Section 1, which includes principles 1-48, covers best practices related to the creative process and the internal issues that most artists confront on a regular basis.

Section 2, which includes principles 49-101, offers a wide range of ways to share, promote, and sell your creative output, as well as grow a fan base.

Pick up this resource whenever you need inspiration or a fresh idea.

Read it straight through or open it randomly to any page. You're bound to find something that will spark a new concept or inspire an action you can take.

You'll get the most out of this book if you read it like you're on a treasure hunt.

There are many rich rewards to be found within these pages. You just have to consume these passion principles with an open mind and an eagerness to put them to good use.

Much success on your creative journey!

Section 1

Express Your Creativity

This section covers best practices related to
the creative process and the internal issues
that most artists confront on a regular basis.

1

Scratch that itch

Sometimes it's subtle; other times it's undeniable. It can feel like a whispering desire or a powerful gravitational pull.

Regardless of what form it takes, it is your creative urge speaking to you.

Don't downplay this impulse. Don't cast it off as frivolous. Take it seriously.

It is the call of your soul, craving to be expressed.

Your job as an artist is to act on that impulse. To feed it and give it the attention it deserves.

Denying your creative desires does a disservice to you and humanity. It stifles your ability to become an authentic expression of who you are.

Listen to your instincts. And scratch that itch!

2

Give yourself the only approval you need

So many artists seek validation.

They think a college degree, a raving review, or high praise from a mentor will justify their creative aspirations.

They want to be acknowledged, so they search in vain for an external green light that gives them permission to move forward.

Here's the truth: The only validation you need is the approval that comes from within.

Looking for self-worth outside yourself is a never-ending quest that leads to permanent frustration.

So right now, this very minute, give yourself permission to be an artist.

Look in the mirror, smile, and say, "I am an artist. I am worthy!"

3

Cultivate a sense of play

Take your creativity seriously, but do so with a sense of ease.

Many artists, writers, musicians, and performers – especially early in their development – work themselves into a paralyzing frenzy when creating.

For instance, do you ever ...

- Stare at a blank canvas, page, or stage and feel frozen?
- Put too much pressure on yourself to create?
- Feel defeated before you even start?

Relax. Creative expression should be fun, not stressful.

Allow yourself the freedom to experiment without judgment.

The fate of the world isn't resting on your ability to craft the perfect sentence, lyric, melody, or punch line.

Life will go on if your first draft doesn't win a Pulitzer, Grammy, or Tony Award.

Have fun. Be light. Cultivate a sense of play.

"Every child is an artist.
The problem is how to remain
an artist once we grow up."

-Pablo Picasso

4

Confront your greatest obstacle

Some artists like to recite a long list of obstacles that keep them from success. They blame culprits such as unsupportive parents, partners, spouses, friends, teachers, etc.

They also curse the dismal local arts scene, the weak economy, the apathetic media, and how society doesn't value art (or music, literature, theatre) anymore.

Yet, at the same time, other artists thrive in this same environment.

Yes, there are challenges along the creative path. And guess where you'll find the most destructive one? Inside your own head.

Your greatest obstacle is self-imposed.

The boogeyman isn't lurking "out there." He resides within, where you have the power to control him.

5

Tell a better story

If you created the internal obstacles that hold you back, you also have the ability to change the narrative in your mind.

What stories do you tell yourself about your role as an artist? And, are those stories serving you or hindering you?

Your attitude and actions are powered by your beliefs.

You develop your beliefs by thinking the same thought repeatedly – whether that thought is good or bad, productive or destructive.

If the story in your head is an empowering one, keep telling it.

But, if that story is holding you back, dismiss it and tell a better story. And tell it repeatedly, until it becomes your new belief about yourself and the world around you.

Compare yourself to the one person who matters

Artists are good at playing the comparison game.

Do you ever wonder how your work stacks up against "the competition"?

No matter how much praise you get, do you worry your craft isn't good enough?

It's great to expose yourself to other artists' work. It's healthy to be inspired by their skills.

But it's a bad idea to use other artists as a measuring stick by which to judge your own value and capabilities.

There's only one person whose quality of work really matters, and that person is you.

Is what you created today satisfying or an improvement on what you created yesterday? If you can answer "yes" most of the time, you're doing great.

"Don't waste time chasing after success or comparing yourself to others. Every flower blooms at a different pace. Excel at doing what your passion is and only focus on perfecting it."

-Suzy Kassem

Embrace the F-word

No matter how much you pump yourself up with confidence, a pesky little monster will still creep up on you.

You know this destructive creature by name. It's the most vulgar word to an artist.

It's the thing that consistently stops creative expression in its tracks.

We're talking, of course, about FEAR!

Artists have the mistaken belief they must banish fear to succeed. That they must become "fearless" to make progress.

Nothing could be further from the truth.

Instead, the most successful artists learn to accept (and even embrace) fear. They acknowledge it and move forward despite its presence in their minds.

Learn to do the same!

Make uncertainty your friend

Along with fear, there's another culprit you must become aware of and embrace. This one goes by many names, but it's best described as "uncertainty."

You know this rascal has you by the throat when you find yourself saying things like, "But I've never done that before!" or "But I have no idea how to do that!"

You know you're a victim when you find yourself paralyzed because you don't know how something will turn out.

Guess what? That's part of being human.

No one knows how anything will turn out – until they actually do it.

There are no guarantees.

You can let that fact scare you or thrill you. The choice is yours.

9

Turn your inner critic into a cartoon

We all have that voice in our head. It's the inner critic.

It speaks to us when fear and uncertainty rise up to make themselves known.

Many artists take that voice seriously. So much so that they give it a megaphone and turn up the volume, which leads to inaction and stagnation.

Here's the best remedy ...

Give your inner critic a ridiculous, cartoon voice. Turn it into a silly character. Give it a zany name.

Imagine those negative thoughts being delivered by a unicorn named Butch, a three-year-old child, or a talking whoopee cushion.

Make it so that you can't possibly take that voice and its message seriously.

Do not fear mistakes.
There are none."

-Miles Davis

10

Put struggle in its proper place

You hear a lot about "struggling" artists. You know, those poor souls who toil for years through the hardship of obscurity.

Sounds romantic, right?

Actually, no. It doesn't sound appealing at all.

It's a notion based on a misguided stereotype.

The truth is, challenges are a part of life. And not just for artists.

Every human struggles at one time or another – even people who pursue prestigious careers in law, medicine, and technology.

Yet creative people get unfairly labeled as "struggling" if success doesn't come quickly. That's nonsense. Don't believe the myth.

Create your own label. How about "thriving artist" or "enthusiastic artist"?

Doesn't that sound better?

11

Decide what success means to you

Creative people often have a narrow view of what it means to "make it." Their definition of success is often based on the well-known people who inspired them.

If your role models include Stephen King, Meryl Streep, or Aretha Franklin, you may always feel like you fall short.

Here's a better approach ...

Create your own definition of success.

Reaching millions of people, making lots of money, and being in the national spotlight would be great. But those things aren't required to do fulfilling work.

Success in the arts is whatever you decide it is.

So strive to make a bigger impact while still being happy with where you are now.

12

Embrace the gap

Ira Glass, host of the public radio show *This American Life*, once talked about the frustration creative people feel in the early years of pursuing a craft.

They are inspired to do art because they have a sense of "taste." But at first their technical skills don't allow them to create at the high level they envision.

He referred to this disparity as "the gap." Every creative person experiences it.

Many people give up during this difficult stage.

The solution, according to Glass:

"Do a huge volume of work. Put yourself on a deadline ... Because it's only by going through a volume of work that you are going to catch up and close that gap."

"If you don't feel stupid half the time, you probably aren't trying hard enough."

-Colin Wright

13

Make time for your art

If doing a volume of work is the best solution for getting better at your craft, guess what your next step is?

That's right. *Make art a priority in your life!*

But don't just make that commitment in your head. Bring it into the real world by designating time on your calendar.

Make creating a regular part of your weekly (and even daily) schedule.

Give it the same priority as doctor appointments and showing up for a day job.

Don't treat your art as something you'll do when you can "get around to it." That time rarely comes.

Block it out on the calendar, then honor that creative commitment!

14

Create a space for your art

Along with carving out time for your craft, also have a dedicated work area.

If you always have to clear a space before you begin, you'll be less likely to act on your commitment to your art.

If you're a painter, have a place where your brushes, paint, and tools are always ready.

If you're a dancer, set up a space where you are free to move.

If you're a musician, make sure you have easy access to your instrument and recording gear.

Writers can be more mobile. Find a local library or coffee shop that appeals to you, and have your laptop ready to go when it's time for your next writing session.

15

Find a balance between process and product

There are times to focus on product (the creative end result you want) and times to focus on process (the technique you use to create).

For instance, if you're a painter commissioned to do a portrait, you keep the client's desires in mind.

If you're an actor rehearsing for a play, you strive to meet the director's vision for their character.

In addition, allot time to create with no end result in mind. Make opportunities to experiment and play with your medium and technique.

Write songs on different instruments. Craft stories from a different point of view. Use unusual materials for your art.

Find a healthy balance between free-flowing experimentation and purposeful creation with an end result in mind.

"A bird doesn't sing because it has an answer. It sings because it has a song."

-Maya Angelou

16

Produce a tangible prototype

Every human-made object started as an idea in someone's mind. This is especially true of all works of art, music, performance, and literature.

Prolific artists then take action on their ideas and do the work necessary to transform their inspiration into a 3D reality.

But there's a lag time between conception and manifestation. It takes discipline to keep working with no tangible evidence to motivate you.

Solution: Create a tangible representation of the end result.

Authors or musicians might print a mockup of their book or album cover. Playwrights or filmmakers might create a poster or playbill.

Placing this prototype in plain view will act as a constant reminder that your idea is taking shape in the real world.

17

Capture your ideas

Sometimes inspiration is slow in coming. Other times it flows nonstop.

No matter how quickly your newest ideas come, have a way to capture them so they don't get lost in the ether.

How many times have you had a flash of insight and told yourself you would remember it? Of course, a few hours later you find yourself cursing because you've forgotten what it was.

Take steps now to remedy that situation.

Carry a notebook with you at all times or use your phone as a recording device.

When inspiration strikes, capture every idea.

You can evaluate them later and use the best ones when the time is right.

18

Create when you're not inspired

You hear a lot about artists being visited by "the muse." Inspiration strikes unexpectedly, like a lightning bolt from heaven.

Make no mistake, when those magical times happen, act on them. Strike while your creativity iron is red hot.

But what happens when you're not inspired? Do you just sit and wait for the next miraculous "eureka" moment?

The most prolific and respected artists make doing the work part of their routine.

The lesson for you: Don't wait for the muse. Take action and thereby create the conditions for inspiration to appear.

The many tips you'll find on the following pages will help you do that.

As poet William Butler Yeats once wrote, "Do not wait to strike till the iron is hot; but make it hot by striking."

"The object isn't to make art;
it's to be in that wonderful state
which makes art inevitable."

-Robert Henri

19

Mix and match methods and influences

It's tough to create something truly original. Most new trends in art, music, and literature put a fresh spin on something that is already familiar.

As you spend time honing your craft, force yourself at times to alter your normal approach.

If you usually brush on thick layers of paint, try a more delicate watercolor treatment.

If straight-ahead rock is your musical style, try writing a slow reggae song instead.

Also, combine genres that don't normally go together. How about a science fiction self-help book? Or a musical power ballad about subatomic particles?

You can discover gold when you expand traditional creative boundaries.

20

Challenge yourself with limitations

Creativity can be thrilling when you face a blank canvas and are free to create whatever you want.

It can also be daunting. When anything is possible, where do you begin?

Sometimes having constraints is a blessing.

What if you had to do a painting using only two primary colors?

Or write a blues song about a toaster in the key of A major?

Or write a 500-word romance story with the opening line, "She rolled her eyes that morning at the post office."

At times, give yourself creative constraints.

Doing so will cause you to focus and use your gifts to flourish within the limitations.

21

Consider what you can add or subtract

Another way to create something new is to break down your craft's components into the most basic elements.

Then ask what would happen if you took one element away or added a new one.

Could you write a murder mystery without a dead body?

Or create a one-act play with no spoken dialogue?

Could you record a folk song by adding a vibraphone or a tuba?

How about enhancing your next photography exhibit with a musical soundtrack?

Examine each element of your creation and consider what would happen if you eliminated it.

Also consider how adding something unexpected would affect it.

Try it. You might be surprised by the result.

"Learn the rules like a pro, so you
can break them like an artist."

-Pablo Picasso

22

Choose something to exaggerate or diminish

Along with adding and subtracting elements, also think about which existing aspects of your art you could emphasize or tone down.

Perhaps your new cookbook could focus on the sugar-free recipes and downplay the Paleo diet aspects. Or vice versa.

You may have a wide variety of wildlife paintings, but perhaps your next art show could zero in on your hummingbird images, thereby giving it a more focused theme.

What if your band dedicated an entire set to Elvis Costello cover songs at your next show?

What if you reduced the role of lawyers and police in your next crime thriller novel?

Consider what you can exaggerate or diminish to create something fresh.

23

Find new ideas using random associations

Here's a fun exercise. Make two lists.

For the first one write down five elements related to your craft. A musician might include "lyrics, melody, piano, emotion, amplifier."

Then write a second list of five randomly chosen words, such as "apple, tire, sunshine, belt, and umbrella."

Next, consider one word from each list and challenge yourself to find a connection and generate ideas.

For instance, "tire" and "emotion" might inspire a song about a road trip. "Sunshine" and "melody" might lead to a happy-sounding chorus. "Umbrella" and "lyrics" might combine to form a song about a rainy day.

You might even combine them all to get an upbeat song about a rainy day during a road trip. Give it a shot!

24

Borrow from the best

The next time you're stuck coming up with an idea for a new painting, song, or short story ... try stealing.

Of course, you should never plagiarize someone else's work. But you can borrow some aspect of it – while maintaining your own voice and style.

A songwriter might borrow a chord progression used by another artist but completely change the rhythm. Or mimic the groove of a popular song but use different chords and vocal melodies.

When done right, the new song sounds nothing like the original tune.

A fiction writer could borrow a plot twist but change the characters and setting.

A visual artist could use similar colors or materials but apply it to a different subject matter.

Borrow creative ideas and make them your own.

"The secret to creativity is knowing
how to hide your sources."

-Unknown

25

Make something old new again

If you're like most artists, you want to forge new paths and be an innovator. Nothing wrong with that.

But there's also something to be said for putting your unique stamp on a style or object from the past.

Can you think of a genre that was popular 20 to 50 years ago that's due for a revival?

Perhaps you could take a grunge rock style and meld it with electronic dance music.

Or what if your novel placed a film noir private investigator in the digital era?

Could you take an old object and turn it into modern art?

Consider the many ways you could take something old and make it new again.

26

Try a new medium or genre

Yes, it's good to develop your own recognizable style.

It's also a good idea to continuously experiment and expand your creative horizons – while remaining true to your core voice.

So, every now and then, force yourself to do something different.

If you usually write murder mysteries, try your hand at science fiction or an action-adventure story.

If you normally lean toward folk music, listen to several ska or reggae tracks. Then write a new song influenced by that style.

If you always paint detailed nature scenes, stretch and do an abstract portrait or still life.

Trying new genres can be surprisingly good for you.

27

Let background sounds inspire you

Some artists work best in a quiet environment. Too many sounds distract them.

Others feel more at home with some type of audio stimulation in the background.

That sonic stimulation can be the hum of voices in a coffee shop, mellow jazz music, rock anthems, birds chirping, waves breaking on a beach, and more.

Experiment with different sounds when you create.

Try instrumental tracks without vocals, symphonic music, film scores, heavy metal, meditation music, and sounds of rain and nature.

You can also change sounds based on the project: rock out on a more aggressive piece and mellow out on a more serene endeavor.

Let the audio in your environment support you.

"You can't use up creativity. The more you use, the more you have."

-Maya Angelou

28

Alter your workspace

Another way to trigger a fresh boost of creative energy is to physically change your workspace.

If the area you create in has become messy, spend an hour or two cleaning it up. Decluttering can help clear your mind too.

If your studio or work area has been the same for years, rearrange it. Shift things around in the room or on your desk.

Can you move to a different room in your house or rent a different space?

Could you temporarily change your workspace for an afternoon or a week?

House sit for someone, rent a cabin in the woods, find a picnic table in the park, or spend time at a cafe or coffee shop.

Change your workspace to get a fresh perspective.

29

Imagine yourself as a conduit

Artists claim that inspiration comes to them in all sorts of ways.

Some say it's their personal vision, while others swear that the song, story, or image comes from a divine source.

Perhaps you already think of yourself as a creative conduit in this manner. Maybe your work feels as if it's being downloaded from a higher realm.

If that doesn't describe you, consider giving it a try.

The next time you create, close your eyes and say a silent prayer. Offer to be a vessel through which a pre-existing idea flows.

Imagine you are simply taking dictation or being guided by a higher power.

This approach isn't for everyone, but it might give you an alternative perspective on creative expression.

30

Create a warm-up ritual

Athletes loosen up and practice the fundamentals before every game.

Actors warm up their bodies and voices before a performance.

It's a ritual most of them do automatically.

Do you have a similar habit for your art? If not, consider creating one.

Choose one or more of the following:

Meditate, pray, dance, stretch, do a breathing exercise, listen to music, read something inspiring – whatever gets your mind, body, and soul ready to work.

If you make this a consistent habit, your warm-up ritual will automatically trigger a response, and your creativity will flow faster than ever before.

"The creative process is a process of surrender, not control."

-Julia Cameron

31

Overcome the resistance to start

Most artists find it easy to create once they are in a state of flow.

When a piece of music, a book chapter, a poem, or a painting is well under way, it's fairly easy to keep the momentum going.

You have the beginnings of an idea taking shape, and your brain gets activated in a quest to flesh it out.

But, to get to that wonderful state, you must first do something that will scare you: *Start!*

Resistance to starting is a major culprit for many creative people.

Therefore, you must slay this beast and be willing to start your next project – even when you don't feel like it.

32

Use the five-minute trick

The reason you hesitate before starting a new project is because you convince yourself you're not ready. You're not up to the task. You don't have the time now. You lack the energy.

Here's an easy solution ...

Tell yourself you will spend five minutes on the new project. Just five quick minutes.

Pick up your guitar. Get out your sketchbook. Warm up your voice. Fire up your software.

If you want to stop after five minutes, great. But more often than not, you'll keep going.

One sentence leads to two. One lyric expands into a verse and chorus. Your scribbles get refined.

Before you know it, you're in the flow of inspired creation.

33

Start before you're ready

To sum up the last two principles, you will rarely feel the time is right to start a new creative project.

Accept the fact that your mind will dream up all sorts of reasons you should wait.

This resistance will rear its ugly head often. It's a part of every artist's existence, so expect it.

The good news is, you can be prepared to deal with this monster. You'll overwhelm it with this new principle to live by:

Start before you're ready!

Not sure what you're doing? *Start anyway!*

Afraid you'll get it wrong? *Start anyway!*

Don't have enough energy to devote to it now? *Start anyway!*

"You sit down at the keyboard and put one word after another until it's done. It's that easy, and that hard."

-Neil Gaiman

34

Create more than you consume

It's great to get inspired by exposing yourself to other people's work.

Reading a book by a favorite author or listening to music by an awe-inspiring artist can be invigorating.

The same can be said for researching a new technique or attending a class to learn a new skill. Taking these actions can be helpful.

But don't let the time you devote to consuming information eclipse the time you spend creating.

Some artists use this type of consumption as an avoidance mechanism. Reading about art makes them feel they are engaged in it.

But they're not.

So, make sure you spend plenty of time in creation mode!

35

Understand the health benefits of creative activity

There's so much more to making art than simply satisfying some frivolous personal desire.

Multiple studies over the years have uncovered many tangible health benefits, including:

- Reducing depression and negative emotions
- Improving mood and fostering a positive self image
- Reducing stress and anxiety
- Renewing brain function and speeding up healing
- Helping to prevent Alzheimer's
- Cultivating friendships and a more active social life

In addition to good nutrition and physical activity, being creative just might be one of the best things you can do to stay healthy and happy.

36

Commit to the long haul

No matter what your creative goals are (getting better at your craft, making money with your art, or simply making a difference in other people's lives), it's going to take time to get there.

Are you committed to that journey?

Sadly, there are no shortcuts. There are no quick fixes.

There's only one guaranteed route to success ...

Every day (or as often as you can) you must pick up that instrument, open the computer file, squeeze some paint onto a palette, or otherwise engage in your craft.

And do it consistently and repeatedly over time.

The world needs what you have to offer. It's well worth committing to the long haul.

"The question isn't who is going to let me; it's who is going to stop me."

-Ayn Rand

37

Celebrate small wins

While it may take a while to reach some of your big-picture goals, it's important to set yourself up for success in the short term too.

You don't have to wait months or years to feel like you've accomplished something with your art.

Structure your long-term projects so you hit a number of milestones along the way.

Divide your goals into specific and measurable stages.

Working on a three-act play?

Pat yourself on the back when a solid outline is created. Rejoice when Act 1 is complete. Treat yourself to dessert when Act 2 is finished. And, throw a party when the third and final act is in the can.

Find reasons to celebrate often!

38

Take short breaks when needed

Being consistent with your creative output long term takes discipline. Hopefully, your commitment to your art is filled with curiosity and passion.

However, there will be times when you hit a wall.

Of course, you can prime the pump by taking action when you don't feel inspired. But, every so often, give yourself permission to take a break.

That break can be as short as a ten-minute walk or as long as a two-week sabbatical.

Don't overdo it, but sometimes clearing your mind and shaking up your routine will do you good. It will allow you to view your work with fresh eyes.

Just make sure to return to the business of making art as soon as you can.

39

Communicate with other humans

The life of an artist can be a solitary one, especially for introverted writers and visual artists.

It's easy to get immersed in your art and find yourself holed up for days at a time.

Dedicating that much alone time to your craft is great, but it's also important to interact with other people on a regular basis.

Human beings thrive on personal connections and community.

Even if you don't consider yourself a "people person," plan regular times to get out of your house or studio.

Meet friends for coffee or a meal. Share what you're working on and be eager to learn what they're up to.

These personal interactions will energize you and help you make better art.

"Overcome the notion that you must be regular. It robs you of the chance to be extraordinary."

-Uta Hagen

40

Take an improv class

Ready to stretch beyond your comfort zone? One powerful way to do that is to learn the art of improvisational comedy.

It's a form of theatre that requires you to make up characters, dialogue, and movement on the spot, based on a simple suggestion.

Does that thought scare you? If so, that's all the more reason to take a class.

Learning improv is not about thinking fast, being funny, or getting it "right."

Improv comedy training will teach you to be in the moment, to be fully present and listen, and to find connections between seemingly unrelated things.

It will also compel you to be silly and reconnect with your childlike sense of play.

Learning these principles will greatly enhance your art – and your life.

41

Hang out with upbeat people

Getting out and interacting with other people is a healthy habit to develop. Even better is choosing to spend time with positive people who will lift you up.

Sure, it's good to vent when you need to get something out of your system. And, if a good friend needs to express their frustration, listen to them.

But make that the exception, not the rule.

Gravitate toward friends and family members who are optimistic.

Seek out people who look for opportunities, not limitations.

Avoid friends who complain and focus on problems instead of proactive solutions.

Spend time with people who encourage you and remind you of your value as an artist.

42

Attend local events and expand your network

As you spend more time honing your craft and creating a body of work, be sure to immerse yourself in the world around you.

Do you know what's happening in your local music, art, literature, or performing arts scene?

Are you part of the creative community?

No matter how you rate your social skills, make it a point to get out and attend arts-related events.

Expose yourself to new people and other forms of expression.

Do your best to strike up conversations and meet people.

One new acquaintance may introduce you to three more, and it snowballs from there.

Get out and get connected!

"Networking is rubbish.
Have friends instead."

-Steve Winwood

43

Become a curious investigator

Perhaps you're not fond of networking. You may feel awkward meeting new people and talking about yourself.

That's fine. Because the best way to get to know new people is to talk about their favorite subject: *them*.

From now on, when you attend events, think of yourself as an investigative journalist. It's your job to learn as much as you can about the individuals in the room.

Beyond making this a fun role-playing game, it will help if you are genuinely curious about people.

Cultivate a sense of wonder.

Who is this person? What's their story? What are they passionate about? Why do they do what they do?

Their answers may surprise and inspire you.

44

Reach out to three people a day

This may be one of the most powerful things you can do to develop relationships. Make a commitment to connect with three people every day.

A phone or live video call will be the most impactful, but even a simple text or email will do.

Who you contact is up to you. However, it might help to pick one person from each of these three categories:

- A personal friend or family member you haven't talked to in a while
- A creative peer you haven't touched base with in a while
- Someone new you send an introductory message to

You don't have to ask for anything. Just let them know you're thinking about them. Ask what they're up to. Even better, ask how you can support a project they're working on.

Three simple connections every day will add up to a lot of goodwill over time.

45

Start a mastermind group

Do this when you're ready to take your creative output to the next level. Identify a handful of proactive creative people you admire and suggest forming a mastermind group.

Agree on a regular meeting time – from one to four times a month. Connect in person, by phone, or via a video conference call.

During your sessions, each member shares the progress they've made since the last meeting.

You can also articulate a current challenge or opportunity and ask for advice.

The feedback you get will be invaluable.

End each meeting by stating what actions you'll take in the coming weeks.

You are a powerful individual. Combining your strengths with the group mind will propel you to even greater heights.

"It's important to surround yourself with people you can learn from."

-Reba McEntire

46

Attend a class or retreat

The best thing you can do for your creativity is to sit down and do the work. But smart artists also know the value of learning from others.

No matter how uniquely gifted you think you are, you can always benefit from another artist's perspective.

So keep an eye out for classes that will help you expand your technique and style.

Go with an open mind. Be willing to learn something new.

You'll also make new connections with the instructor and other students.

When you're ready to take a deeper dive, consider going on a weekend or week-long retreat.

Immerse yourself in learning, playing, and meeting new creative people.

47

Support other artists

Once you've been out there for a while meeting artists, teachers, and other creative types, you'll build a network of people who may someday support you.

Just know that support moves in two directions.

In addition to receiving praise and recognition, be eager to give it.

Treat other musicians, writers, actors, and artists as you like to be treated. Take an interest in their work. Compliment them, attend their events, recommend them, and share links to their activities online.

And do so because you think they deserve it, without an expectation that they'll return the favor.

However, if you make supporting other artists a habit, you'll find it will come back to you many times over.

48

Don't quit your day dream

You pursue your craft because you have a calling.

An invisible force compels you to take action, experiment, and turn your ideas into something tangible.

That's fantastic, and hopefully that impulse will fuel your progress for years to come.

However, there will inevitably be slumps, disappointments, and results you may not be happy with. It's fine to acknowledge them, but don't let them throw you off the path for long.

Know that a life in the arts will be a roller coaster ride.

But you'll be fine, as long as you stay focused on your destiny and legacy as a one-of-a-kind creative person.

"Let the beauty of what you
love be what you do."

-Rumi

Section 2

Share Your Creativity

This section offers a wide range of ways
to share, promote, and sell your creative
output, as well as grow a fan base.

"Be who you are and say what you feel, because those who mind don't matter and those who matter don't mind."

–Dr. Seuss

49

Get comfortable with sharing

Some artists are eager to show the world everything they create.

Others are selective and want to display only their best work.

Many cling to their creations and are intimidated by the prospect of being judged and possibly ridiculed.

Which one best describes you?

If you're open to the idea of sharing your work, that's great.

If you're reluctant, know that your feelings are normal. Many artists feel exposed and vulnerable revealing their work.

Exposing your work is something you'll need to get on friendly terms with if you want to truly make an impact with your art.

So, do yourself a favor and warm up to the idea of sharing.

50

Become an inspiration curator

Here's a great way to build an audience early on, before you have a large body of your own work to share.

Get in the habit of regularly posting links to your favorite writers, artists, musicians, and performers.

Seek out the best videos, podcasts, articles, and tutorials on topics related to your art form, and generously share them.

People will come to view you as a trusted source for high-quality information on your creative area of expertise.

This will attract people interested in your core topic and pave the way for when you are ready to promote more of your own work.

Start sharing in this way now.

51

Show your babies

In the early stages of honing your craft, you may want to keep your songs, stories, paintings, and other output to yourself.

After all, you're exploring and learning the ropes.

But at some point, you'll give birth to a finished product you feel good about. That's a great time to put it out there for others to see.

Don't solicit a book publisher or an art gallery. Simply make it available for people to consume.

Post it online as a photo, blog post, video, or audio file that your friends and current followers can sample.

There's no need to boast or ask for a sale. Just show your work.

You might be surprised by the response.

"Make stuff you love, talk about stuff you love, and you'll attract people who love that kind of stuff. It's that simple."

-Austin Kleon

52

Share your process

Believe it or not, art enthusiasts (and even other artists) love to see how creative people do what they do.

Therefore, one simple way to start showing your work is to let people in on your creative process.

Write an article or make a video explaining how you write songs, prepare for a performance, write a first draft, or do an initial sketch.

Give people a peek behind the curtain. It may be mundane to you, but it will be fascinating to many others.

What if you're still figuring out your process? Be honest about that and share your journey of discovery.

You just might attract an audience while doing it.

53

Tell the story behind your art

In addition to sharing how you create, also explain *why* you were motivated to work on a particular piece.

What was the inspiration for your most recent song, poem, stage play, recipe, or photograph?

Storytelling is a powerful way to communicate any message. Use it to draw people in and give deeper insight into your work.

Your fans will feel more of a connection when they know the story behind your creative work. It brings meaning and context to their relationship with your art.

The tale doesn't have to be earth-shattering. Even a frivolous inspiration can be interesting.

Now is a good time to start telling the story behind your art.

54

Start a domino effect

Many artists think that all this business of sharing their work is overly self-serving. It feels like it's "All about me!"

That's one way to look at it. Here's another way:

The world is filled with people who have creative itches they are reluctant to scratch. Many of these people are quite talented and make art that has the potential to change lives.

But they downplay their worth and keep their gifts to themselves.

When you unapologetically express yourself and share your work, you inspire other artists to take a chance and do the same.

You lead by example and create a ripple effect of artistic expression. You end up serving humanity in a powerful way.

So get over it and start sharing!

"Our chief want is someone who will inspire us to be what we know we could be."

-Ralph Waldo Emerson

55

Teach what you do in person

If you've been working on your craft for a year or two, you most likely have all the skills necessary to teach what you do.

Even if you feel like you're still a novice, you know a lot more than someone who is just getting started.

In fact, catering to beginners is the best way to start teaching.

There's a huge market of newcomers wanting to learn how to play guitar, sing, paint, act, use recording equipment, and more.

Find a local space where you can offer classes and promote your new endeavor.

Teaching gets you immersed in your field.

It also helps you make money, develop an early fan base, and become a better artist.

56

Teach what you do online

Once you have some experience teaching face to face in a live setting, your next step may be teaching online.

Why limit yourself to students who live in your immediate area?

There are many ways to become an online educator.

You can teach one-on-one using Skype or some similar video conferencing service.

You can teach via webinars or live video streaming.

If you learn some basic video production skills, you could create an online course that students take at their own pace.

You can charge for these courses to earn extra income or offer them free to build an audience. The choice is yours.

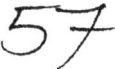

Encourage questions (and answer them)

Here's another smart thing you can do if you teach and share your creative process.

Solicit questions from your followers and students. Also, notice the questions you get most often regarding your craft.

Then set up a forum to address those questions on a regular basis.

You can answer them through a series of videos, blog posts, audio podcasts, or live meet-ups.

Building a library of questions and answers will position you as an expert on your creative topic.

That's right. You'll be more than just an artist; you'll become an artistic source of inspiration, too!

So, start encouraging questions.

"Creativity is a type of learning process where teacher and pupil are located in the same individual."

-Arthur Koestler

58

Interview people in your creative field

Here's a potent way to attract new followers, especially if you are just starting out or feel you aren't ready to play the "expert" role yet.

Reach out to artists you admire and offer to interview them.

The format can be text-based, audio, or video. Post a new interview weekly and make it an ongoing series.

Also seek out authors and other experts in your field.

Once you've published dozens of interviews, you'll have the clout to go after bigger names. The more popular the person and topic, the more attention you'll receive.

If you dedicate yourself to an interview series, you'll see results.

59

Commit to a regular schedule of sharing

No matter what type of sharing you choose to do online or in person, commit to being consistent with your output.

Whether you teach, share your process, interview other artists, answer questions, or publish a blog, podcast, or video channel ... do it on a regular schedule.

Decide what you can reasonably handle: weekly, twice a month, monthly? Every Monday and Thursday?

Pick a frequency and stick with it.

Sporadic output will create sporadic results. Consistency will help you stay on track and more quickly build an audience for the unique type of material you share.

Dedicate yourself to becoming a consistent sharing machine!

60

Lead a retreat

If you have some modest success teaching live in your area, or if you build a decent online following, consider offering a more substantial live event.

Retreats have become popular because they offer attendees an opportunity to get away and immerse themselves in a chosen activity.

These events can take place over a weekend, a few days, or an entire week or more.

Could you lead a retreat on your art form? Or could you collaborate with other artists and experts and put one together?

Come up with a theme, find a location, set a date, and determine a price. Then promote it and see what happens.

It might be a fulfilling way to serve your fans and followers.

"If your actions inspire others to dream more, learn more, do more, and become more, you are a leader."

-John Quincy Adams

61

Offer arts-related tours

Do you live in an area that has a rich cultural history?

Or are you fascinated by a region of the world that has an arts-related identity?

Consider conducting group tours.

This would especially work well if your city has a storied history of music, art, dance, food, or literature.

You just might find an appreciative audience of people eager to learn more about landmarks, childhood homes of well-known figures, etc.

If you're more adventurous, you could organize group trips to destinations that fascinates you. Perhaps Memphis, Sedona, London, Paris, or Fiji.

What topics and locations light you up? And how could you connect with and serve other people who share that same passion?

62

Start a movement

Most human beings flourish when they are part of a community. People thrive when they feel connected to a tribe of like-minded individuals.

Sometimes these groups form organically based on shared interests, backgrounds, and goals.

The most engaged tribes, though, are inspired by a leader. Someone with a well-defined vision or an admired skill attracts people to their cause.

As an artist, you can join an existing community as a follower. Or, you can become the leader of your own tribe.

It will help if you have a clear mission and think beyond just an area of shared interest.

Turn your passion into a movement and lead your community to greater heights.

63

Describe what you do in an interesting way

It's the age-old question: "So, what do you do?"

Whether you're at a party, a networking event, a conference, or in line at the grocery store, you will encounter this familiar question.

How will you answer it?

Most artists get caught off guard and mumble something like, "I dabble in writing" or "I'm a struggling songwriter."

Neither of those are very interesting or empowering. Take pride in what you create.

Consider these alternative responses: "I shoot family portraits in exotic locations" or "I write romance novels for adventurous women."

However you answer, strive to be confident and intriguing. Say something unexpected that leads people to ask, "Tell me more about that."

"Take advantage of every opportunity to practice your communication skills so that when important occasions arise, you will have the gift, the style, the sharpness, the clarity, and the emotions to affect other people."

- Jim Rohn

64

Understand the role of
fans and supporters

There are many factors that determine a creative person's level of success: talent, determination, connections, marketing savvy, a large body of work, etc.

But if your goal is monetary success and popularity, one factor stands above the rest:

Having a sizable number of admirers who support you with their time, attention, presence, and money.

Sure, being excellent at your craft and having lots of industry connections are great. But those things won't bring you cash flow and impact.

Only a supportive group of fans will deliver the goods.

Your creative journey will be greatly enhanced if you make building relationships with fans a regular habit that you enjoy.

65

Build an audience first

Here's the typical pattern that artists follow:

They work on a new album, book, play, or video for months.

Then they release it and realize they need to "market it." Then they bombard their friends and followers with sales announcements.

Sadly, this is not very effective and can alienate many people.

Try this instead: Start sharing your message now, before you have anything to sell.

Post interesting things about your craft, process, story, journey, etc. And do it only with an intention to inform and inspire people.

Build an audience interested in your topic first. Then, when you have something to promote, you'll have an existing fan base to share it with.

66

Preach to the choir

Many creative people think of promoting their work as a battle.

They go to war to grab people's attention and make an unsuspecting public aware of their latest offering.

It's a battle fraught with challenges. Interrupting people with marketing messages and converting them into customers is hard work.

There's an easier way, and no convincing or manipulation is required.

Simply determine who already wants what you offer. Who is currently hungry for what you create?

In other words, stop trying to convert people. Preach to the choir instead! Go for the low-hanging fruit of potential fans.

Who is predisposed to like you? And how can you more easily reach them?

"At the end of the day, it's the fans who make you who you are."

-Chris Cornell

67

Decide who your tribe is

Whether you're simply attracting fans or leading a bigger movement, it helps to have a clear idea who you're catering to.

Ideally, what type of person do you want to commune with? Who is your tribe?

Of course, not all supporters will fit into a cookie-cutter category. But you will discover patterns and similarities.

Create a profile of your perfect fan.

Consider many factors when describing them: age range, gender, life experiences, political leanings, spiritual inclinations, geography, ethnic background, causes they support, etc.

Quite often, your ideal tribe member is a lot like you.

Having a clear idea who your most fervent supporters are will help you attract more of them.

68

Determine where your tribe hangs out

Creating a profile of your ideal fan is an important step. Next, you'll need to determine the best ways to communicate with them.

To do that, it'll help to know where you can find these good people.

So, take a look at the description you came up with in the last principle. Then answer these questions:

- Where do they get their news and entertainment?
- Where do they shop and hang out?
- What online destinations do they frequent?
- What communities are they a part of?
- What activities do they participate in?

Your answers to these questions are a gold mine. They reveal clues to the best ways to connect with new fans and supporters.

69

Build an email list

Knowing there are people who appreciate your work is great.

However, if you truly want to impact your fans' lives on a deeper level, you'll need to communicate with them directly.

Having a website and social media presence are ways to do that, but the most powerful communication tool you will ever have is a mailing list.

That's why the most savvy artists regularly encourage people to subscribe to their email list. And they do it in a way that's enticing and benefit-driven.

They offer incentives, like free downloads and exclusive perks. They ask fans to join their "community," not their "list."

You'd be wise to do the same.

"I think my fans will follow me
into our combined old age.
Real musicians and real fans stay
together for a long, long time."

-Bonnie Raitt

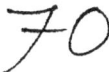

Reach out to your list regularly

Building your fan list and using an email service provider (there are many good ones out there) are essential steps to sharing your work.

But having a list and a system won't amount to anything unless you use them.

Communicating with your digital community must become a regular activity. Put it on your calendar and send something to your supporters at least once or twice a month.

Share your latest projects and adventures.

If you don't have anything new to report, share a link to someone else's work related to your art form.

Stay in front of your fans. Send them funny, helpful, or inspiring messages, in addition to promotional items.

71

Seek out open mics, CFAs, and more

Are you ready to share your art in the real world? Then start looking for the many opportunities that are out there.

If you do music, poetry, or performance art, most cities have at least one open mic night.

Art galleries, coffee shops, and businesses often put out a call for artists (CFA) when looking for new talent to display. Some have a submission fee; others don't.

Free classified sites, like Craigslist, usually have listings from venues looking for musicians, bands, visual artists, and more.

You may also find script readings and events where comics, playwrights, and actors can try out new material.

Opportunities exist all around you. You just have to make time to search for them.

72

Look for alternative spaces

Every creative field has its traditional venues.

For musicians it's concert halls. For visual artists it's galleries. For actors it's professional theaters. For authors it's bookstores.

That's great, but those aren't the only games in town. Think outside the established box and find unexpected locations to perform or show your work.

Consider malls, public parks, private homes, warehouses, cafes, coffee shops, specialty retail stores, neighborhood block parties, or the back of a pickup truck.

Expand your concept of potential places to reach a live audience.

Where do lots of people congregate in your area? Where do your ideal fans hang out?

Approach the people who run those places and explore the possibilities.

"If opportunity doesn't
knock, build a door."

-Milton Berle

73

Brainstorm ideas for a themed event

Live events can be powerful. When someone experiences your music, art, or performance in the flesh, they are more likely to feel a connection with you.

But not all events are created equal. Some have more drawing power than others.

One way to make an event stand out is to give it a theme.

A tribute to Johnny Cash, a night of female stand-up comics, or an art exhibit inspired by Star Trek has the potential to attract more people than a generic music, comedy, or art show.

By narrowing the scope, the theme acts like a magnet for a targeted audience. It makes the event unique.

What themes might work for you?

74

Collaborate with your peers

Many artists think of other musicians, writers, and creatives as competition.

"It's a dog-eat-dog world," they say. Every artist needs to look out for number one: themselves.

But that's a short-sighted view.

A better approach is to collaborate with your creative peers.

Instead of one painter putting on an exhibition, why not organize a group show where five artists work together to draw a crowd?

All five benefit from the effort, and all get exposure to the other artists' friends and fans.

Instead of being afraid to share your audience with other artists, open up to the overall goodwill you create.

Over time, that inclusive attitude will benefit you greatly.

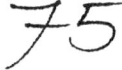

Throw a party

Live events come in all shapes and sizes. Music concerts, art shows, film screenings, book signings, etc.

Many are quite traditional and expected.

So, do something creative to stand apart. Instead of planning your next gig, exhibit, or performance ... consider throwing a party.

Especially when you don't have a new book, album, play, or film to promote, find a reason to celebrate anyway.

People love being invited to events where they'll have fun, meet interesting people, and experience something different.

So create that opportunity for them.

Decorate the venue, plan a fun activity, add live music or performance art.

Make it a party that people will be excited about before, during, and after the event.

"The reason you dance and sing
is to make the audience feel like
they're dancing and singing.
As long as you're having fun
and giving it 100 percent,
they're gonna feel that too."

-Heath Ledger

76

Take it to the streets

Art, music, and literature have never been limited to galleries, concert venues, and bookstores.

Creative people have an infinite number of ways to share their work.

One effective way is to express themselves in public places.

Musicians can perform on sidewalks, street corners, or in front of supportive businesses.

Visual artists can post graffiti or paint murals on the sides of buildings.

Filmmakers can screen movies in a parking lot under the stars.

Writers can recite poetry or do readings in a park or by a lake.

Some of these activities require a license or permission, but they are all worth exploring.

77

Hold a fundraiser

Art can serve humanity in many ways. One of the best ways to attract attention and support a good cause is to organize a fundraising event.

People love to donate to charities, nonprofits, and families that need financial help.

Therefore, when you become aware of an organization whose mission you are passionate about, or a family in need, consider holding a fundraiser.

Ideally, the recipient of the funds will be eagerly involved in your event. They'll spread the word to their friends and supporters, and you'll make your fans aware of the good cause.

It's also easier to get media exposure for fundraisers, so it becomes a win on many fronts.

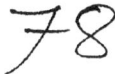

Become a positive influence

Many creative people look at their city and find all sorts of things to complain about.

They bemoan how the art galleries, music venues, bookstores, and theatre companies do too little of this or too much of that.

These artists thrive on finding fault and placing blame.

There's a better way:

Instead, ask what you can do to make your local arts community stronger and more interesting.

Could you host a local artist support group? Or organize an exciting collaborative event that would create positive buzz?

Proactive artists don't just sing a chorus of complaints. They offer solutions and find ways to make a contribution to the communities in which they live, work, and play.

"What you do makes a difference,
and you have to decide what kind
of difference you want to make."

-Jane Goodall

79

Ask this simple, mind-expanding question

Some artists compartmentalize their creativity.

They can easily apply expansive thinking and innovation to their craft. However, when it comes to sharing their work with the public, they suddenly become close-minded.

The most successful creative people are visionaries in many areas.

One simple way to generate great ideas for exposing your art is to ask, "What would happen if ...?"

Think big. Be silly. Get outrageous. Use ideas from other industries.

What would happen if you ... wrote a music jingle for a popular morning radio show? Or put together a kazoo marching band? Or encouraged fans to dress like superheroes at your next show?

See how much fun this can be?

80

Drip out your work

The traditional approach to creativity is to hole up for months or years as you work on a new project.

A collection of your best work is eventually released as a full-length music album, novel, nonfiction book, art or photo exhibit, fashion line, film, stage play, etc.

Here's another option: Drip out your newest creations piecemeal, one item at a time.

There's no need to wait till an entire album is done. Instead, share your latest song now. Then write, record, and share another one next month.

You can do the same with paintings, short stories, sketch comedy, jewelry, and more. This pattern also helps you get more consistent exposure throughout the year.

Consider dripping out your work a little at a time.

81

Create your own vehicle

Many creative people look around their hometown and search for things the city can do for them.

Other artists seek out mentors, gatekeepers, media people, managers, and agents in an effort to gain "credibility" that will lift them out of obscurity and make them feel worthy.

Want to know what the most empowered artists do? They *create* the circumstances they're looking for.

If venues aren't booking you, find a cafe or retailer that wants more patrons and work together to create an event.

If the media isn't covering you, launch your own blog, podcast, or YouTube channel and broadcast your story yourself.

Stop waiting to be discovered.

Start orchestrating your own lucky breaks.

"The people who get on in this world are the people who get up and look for the circumstances they want, and, if they can't find them, make them."

-George Bernard Shaw

82

Use your wins as stepping stones

If you're an ambitious creative person, you're probably impatient. You want to make progress and see results sooner rather than later.

That's great. It means you have drive, and that quality will serve you well.

However, if your next victory in the art world is a small one, don't downplay it. As was suggested earlier, celebrate the win.

More important, use that positive baby step to fuel your next move. Let it fill you with confidence and determination.

Consider what you learned from the experience. Then leverage the mini victory to reach for a bigger, more significant outcome.

Every achievement along the path prepares you for the next stage of the creative journey.

83

Seek out publicity

There's a lot you can do on your own to create awareness for your work and connect with fans.

But it's also nice when you get a boost of recognition from a media source that caters to your ideal audience.

Therefore, regularly think about how your art and your personal story might be *newsworthy.*

Is there a newspaper, magazine, radio show, TV station, or website that is perfectly aligned with what you're currently doing?

Don't just think about the largest media entity you'd like to be covered in. What's the best fit for your story?

You'll get more media coverage when you find the overlap between an outlet's format and what you can deliver to their audience.

84

Tie into trends

One great way to improve your chances of getting publicity is to tie into a current trend or topic in the news.

It's also an effective way to attract attention in general.

Beware though. Don't jump on just any hot topic.

Make sure it dovetails with your form of artistic expression or is a subject you feel strongly about.

For instance, the weeks before Valentine's Day would be a great time to talk about romance and love songs, if that's what you write and perform.

If you've overcome a major illness or life challenge (and if you express that experience through your art), be willing to share your perspective the next time that topic is in the news.

"I really appreciate when people use their fame and voice for more than just self-promotion, starting a dialogue about a topic or an issue much bigger than themselves."

-Questlove

85

Follow up

Silence. You'll encounter it whether you pursue media coverage, music gigs, freelance work, or simply want to connect with a respected person in your field.

You leave a voice mail or send an email. Then you wait. And wait. A reply doesn't come.

Most artists assume that silence equals rejection – a deafening "No!"

However, that may not be the case at all.

Many of the people you attempt to reach are busy and distracted. So with all of your communications, be prepared to send at least one or two follow-up messages.

Be pleasant at all times. Present yourself as a perk, not a pest. And follow up.

You just might be surprised by the results.

86

Create an online hub for your work

These days it's so easy to set up free profiles on social media sites and apps, there's a good chance you haven't created your own website.

That's understandable. You want to set up shop where the most people are congregating.

But the truth is, these free sites don't owe you anything.

They own the platform and all the data on your friends and followers. They can take it away from you at any time, for any reason.

That's why it's smart to also have an online destination you control. You want to own the domain name and site where all of your music, art, or books reside.

This online hub is the primary place you send people to learn more about your work.

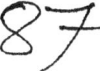

Get visual online

The digital world we live in is multi-sensory. Using only a smartphone, people can read, watch, or listen to a wide variety of content.

To stand out in this oversaturated multimedia era, you need to grab attention. One of the best ways to do that is to add a visual element to most of the things you share online.

The occasional text update is fine. But more often than not, add a striking photo or image of some type.

Authors can post book covers or photos from public events.

Musicians can post images of live performances, studio sessions, or life on the road.

Artists can post their paintings or photos, along with shots of their workspace.

The possibilities are endless, so get visual.

"The more strikingly visual your presentation is, the more people will remember it."

-Paul Arden

Have a consistent look and message

You know this by now. To make a long-lasting impact with your talent, you must be in it for the long haul.

An important element of this marathon journey is consistency – especially with the things you share in public.

Yes, you can experiment and evolve as an artist. At the same time, you can also emphasize your unique style and voice.

Strive to emit a recognizable theme, which can include:

- How you dress in photos and at live events
- The attitude and worldview you express
- The look of your visuals
- The sound of your music
- The frequency of your communication
- The brand identity you broadcast

All of these things reinforce who you are and what you create.

89

Get comfortable on camera

One of the most potent ways to express yourself in the digital era is with video. People the world over are consuming video content at unprecedented rates.

If you're not using video regularly, now would be a great time to start.

You don't have to be on camera yourself to make good use of video, but it would be beneficial to get comfortable speaking into a camera lens.

You can use either live streaming or prerecorded video to share your live events, virtual concerts, commentaries, tips, studio tours, interviews, and more.

If you feel uncomfortable with how you look and sound on video, you can get better at it. It just takes practice. So start learning now.

90

Run low-cost ads

There are many no-cost ways to promote yourself organically online. With the right message and persistence, those free avenues can be effective.

However, many artists have found they can extend their reach with well-placed paid ads.

For a small investment, you can have your social media messages show up as "sponsored" updates or "promoted posts," which are seen by more people.

The good news is, you can have these paid ads served up to highly specific types of people.

This is not old-school shotgun advertising. These days you can target by gender, age, geography, personal interests, and more.

Bottom line: Consider spending a little money on these low-cost ad options.

"Branding demands commitment –
commitment to continual re-invention,
striking chords with people to stir
their emotions, and commitment
to imagination."

-Sir Richard Branson

91

Create magnetic titles

We live in an increasingly multimedia-driven world, with a proliferation of visual and audio content online.

Still, when people search for things, they use words. Simple text.

In response to that, search engines and social media sites deliver relevant results for whatever topic is being queried.

That's why it's so important to clearly label all of your online content. Make sure your titles and descriptions spell out what the video, blog post, or podcast is about.

Avoid being cute, clever, or vague.

Consider the words and phrases people will use to search for this type of information. Then include those words in your title, description, and tags.

Brushing up on search engine optimization (SEO) tips like this will serve you well.

92

Repurpose what you share

Many artists get discouraged when they share their work and other messages online – especially when it comes to creating fresh content and staying in the public eye.

It can be exhausting to crank out new tips, updates, photos, videos, and more every week.

Here's some good news: You don't have to reinvent the wheel every time.

For starters, the same video or link you post to one site can be published to several others. In addition, consider transforming everything you create into multiple formats.

A written article can be turned into a spoken-word audio podcast. That audio can be combined with images and turned into a video. Take a quote or tip from the article and incorporate it into a photo.

Use your artist's brain to explore the many possibilities.

93

Ask for the sale

This is a tough one for many artists.

To begin with, there's so much emotional baggage around the topic of money. Naming a price and encouraging a sales transaction can further complicate things.

But if you want to be a professional artist, you must move through the discomfort and get on friendlier terms with sales.

Get in the habit of using a "call to action." It can be as simple as "This new painting is available for sale. Let me know if you're interested."

Come right out and ask people to buy your products or attend your events. Not all the time. Up to a third of your updates and emails can include such requests.

Don't be overly timid and hope people buy from you. Ask them!

"People buy because they want to enhance their lives. Because what they see reminds them of something. Because there's a story behind the art or the artist."

-Roger Cummiskey

94

Focus on WIIFT

Here's the great news about marketing and selling your music, books, art, crafts, plays, food, fashion, and more:

It's not about you. It's all about the buyer, the supporter, the fan.

Keep this acronym in mind when marketing: WIIFT.

It stands for "what's in it for them." Always focus on the benefit the other person receives from your art.

How do your biggest fans feel when they interact with your creative goods? What emotional payoff do they get?

Highlight that feeling!

In other words, promote the experience, not the product.

It helps to have a firm understanding of the value your art delivers. Once you embrace that, marketing and sales get a lot easier.

95

Share the praise

Hopefully, when you get positive feedback about your work, it makes you feel good. It's personally satisfying to know your art has touched someone.

There's no need to keep those kind words to yourself.

When you share the praise you receive from fans, the media, or respected people in your field, it offers a form of social proof.

It demonstrates that your work is making an impact.

If someone offers a meaningful compliment in an email or private conversation, ask for permission to use it as a testimonial.

If they publicly post a glowing review or comment, share it right away or grab a digital "screen shot" image to use later.

Let people know how others are benefiting from your art.

96

Ask your fans what they want

Your ultimate inspiration for the work you create obviously comes from within.

In addition to that, once you have even a small following, you can tap into your fans' desires too.

Your supporters let you know what resonates with them whenever they spend money on you or express their praise.

Pay attention to that valuable feedback.

However, you can also be proactive and ask what they would like to see, hear, read, taste, and experience more of.

That doesn't mean you have to cater to every whim. But knowing what your fans want can lead to more inspired work.

And that knowledge will help you make a bigger difference in the world.

"You've got to ask! Asking is the world's most powerful – and neglected – secret to success and happiness."

-Percy Ross

97

Identify your super supporters

You've probably heard of the 80/20 rule.

It accurately predicts that 80 percent of your sales come from 20 percent of your customers. Or that 80 percent of your positive word-of-mouth buzz is generated by 20 percent of your fans.

In other words, your most enthusiastic supporters make up a small percentage of your overall fan base.

It's your job to become aware of who those super fans are, and then spend extra time nurturing relationships with them.

Thank the good people who support you. Surprise them with kind gestures and simple gifts. Publicly acknowledge them.

They are the lifeblood of your creative career. Treat them accordingly.

98

Ask for help

Artists are afraid to ask for help because they think it makes them appear needy. Or they're worried that the requested activity will be a burden to other people.

The truth is, when you approach the right people in the right way, they're often honored that you thought enough of them to ask.

Some will even wonder why you didn't ask sooner.

You can ask for help in any number of areas: generating ideas, proofreading material, pinning up posters, setting up for events, working the door, spreading the word, running sound, and more.

Move past your reluctance to seek support.

Let people know what you need ... and ask for help.

99

Be someone people want to work with

As you become a more proactive artist, people will be drawn to work with you for all sorts of reasons.

Some will be attracted to your talent, clout, popularity, or confidence.

But there's another, even more important reason: how easy you are to work with.

When someone hires you or collaborates with you in some way, what do they experience?

Is it joy and satisfaction? Or regret and frustration? Do they feel lifted up or weighed down?

You must become hyper aware of how you show up and play with others.

The more pleasant the experience you help create, the more opportunities will come your way.

"Work hard, be kind, and
amazing things will happen."

-Conan O'Brien

100

Care about people

The most successful and influential musicians, writers, and artists display a wide range of qualities.

One of the most common and important traits is a sincere desire to be a positive influence in the world.

People are drawn to artists who care.

Your impact will grow significantly if you genuinely care about:

- Fans who support you
- People who run and staff the venues that showcase your talent
- Members of the media and others who spread your message
- People who compliment your work and encourage you

Yes, you must tend to your personal needs and creative desires. At the same time, be sure to spend an equal amount of energy on other people.

101

Express your gratitude

This final passion principle is best implemented by uttering two simple words on a regular basis. Here they are ...

Thank you!

It seems easy enough, but some artists forget to stop and express their gratitude to the people who support and encourage them.

Be different. Thank people often. Make it a ritual. Let people know how much you appreciate them. And do it sincerely.

Your gifts and talents mean so much more when other people are touched by your work.

Your legacy and creative influence require the active participation of others.

So express your gratitude. Every day.

To everyone who needs to hear it.

Final Thoughts

You can learn a lot by simply observing nature.

Whether you look at miniscule microorganisms or the vast expanse of galaxies across the universe, there seems to be an evolutionary impulse at work.

The world is powered by a force that favors growth, expansion, and creation.

In this context, your urge to make music, literature, art, or anything else is not some whimsical, self-indulgent pursuit. It's actually part of the essential role you play in the miraculous cosmic mystery.

It's an instinct within you that emanates from the life-giving intelligence that created you.

Bottom line: You have an intrinsic need to create, to express, to grow, and to influence the world around you.

Don't take that impulse lightly.

Embrace the artist in you. Use the principles throughout this book to express your gifts and share them with the world.

By design, you have a creative spark within. *Ignite it and let it shine!*

Special Recognition Section

Thanks to the following people for being beta readers and providing the valuable feedback that made this a much better book:

Linda Austin	Cathy Yost	Betty Gleason
Peter Mulraney	Jordan Anderson	Martin Thomas
Michelle Humphrey	Chris Martins	Lizbeth Friedman
Angelo Furlan	Mishy Katz	Michael Plishka
Dennis Deschamps	Emily A. Filmore	Joshua Liston
Heidi McCurdy	David Ford	Kathy Gerstorff
Billy Grisack	Mary Lemanski	Steve Wickenton
Marva Lord	Luke Harnett	Eirinn Fraser
Nancy Nigh	Robin Brock	Dustin Plegge
Mike Neuman	Kim-Char Meredith	Deepak Morris
Michael Harrison	Jeanne Felfe	Facundo Alvarez
Monique DeMoulin	Joseph Biener	Matt Denton
Linda Senn	Dibakar Bala	John Henry Sheridan
Allie Oliver-Burns	Christine Rose	Kevin Hahn
Star Cummings	Bill Carter	Fernando Bartolome Zofio

Also by Bob Baker

The Empowered Artist: A Call to Action for Musicians, Writers, Visual Artists, and Anyone Who Wants to Make a Difference With Their Creativity

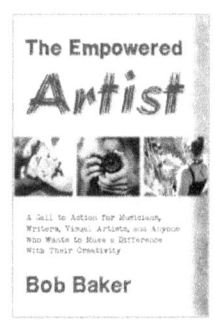

The DIY Career Manifesto: The Unconventional Guide to Turning Your Talents and Know-How Into a Profitable Business

Unleash the Artist Within: Four Weeks to Transforming Your Creative Talents into More Recognition, More Profit and More Fun

Branding Yourself Online: 10 Steps to Creating a Potent Personal Brand Identity on the Internet

The Improv Comedy Musician: The Ultimate Guide to Playing Music with an Improv Group (with Laura Hall)

Guerrilla Music Marketing Handbook: 201 Self-Promotion Ideas for Songwriters, Musicians and Bands on a Budget

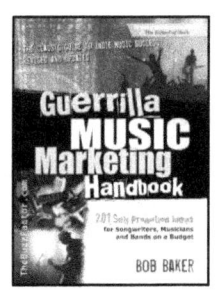

The Five-Minute Music Marketer: 151 Easy Music Promotion Activities That Take 5 Minutes or Less

The 9 Irrefutable Laws of Music Marketing

Guerrilla Music Marketing Online: 129 Free and Low-Cost Strategies to Promote & Sell Your Music on the Internet

19 Cash Flow Strategies for Musicians and Bands

The Guerrilla Guide to Book Marketing: Laying the Foundation for Indie Author Success

Book Marketing Online: The Guerrilla Guide to Building Your Author Platform

Mega Book Publicity: 5 Steps to Getting Free Media Exposure for Your Books

21-Day Abundance and Money Attraction Brain Boost

Learn more about Bob's ...

Marketing tips for songwriters, musicians, and bands
www.TheBuzzFactor.com

Advice for independent authors and book publishers
www.FullTimeAuthor.com

Improv comedy classes and shows
www.ImprovSTL.com

Upbeat original music
www.SoulMassageMusic.com

Original paintings and artwork
www.PopRockArtStudio.com

Connect with Bob

By email:

bob@bob-baker.com

On social media:

www.Twitter.com/MrBuzzFactor

www.YouTube.com/MrBuzzFactor

www.Facebook.com/BobBakerFanPage

www.Instagram.com/mrbuzzfactor

www.Linkedin.com/in/buzzfactor

www.Google.com/profiles/MrBuzzFactor

Free Gifts for You!

As a special thank you for purchasing this book, I want to give you free access to my course, "30 Ways to Become an Empowered Artist."

You'll get more than three hours of online video training that will help you become a more confident and prosperous artist.

I'll also send you a free sample of my book, *The DIY Career Manifesto: The Unconventional Guide to Turning Your Talents and Know-How Into a Profitable Business*.

Just head to this website to claim these free gifts now:

www.PromoteYourCreativity.com

www.ingramcontent.com/pod-product-compliance
Lightning Source LLC
Chambersburg PA
CBHW072034190526
45165CB00017B/679